Bernadette Fitzgerald   Kay Hiatt   Joyce Hilyer

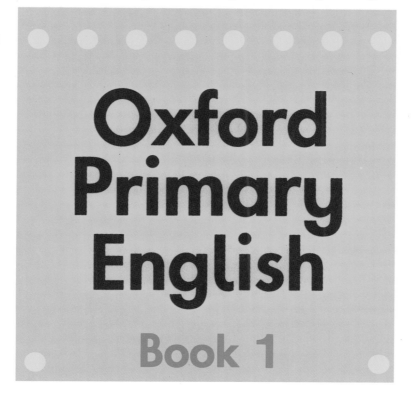

Oxford
Primary
English

Book 1

Oxford University Press

Oxford University Press, Walton Street, Oxford OX2 6DP

Oxford New York Toronto
Delhi Bombay Calcutta Madras Karachi
Kuala Lumpur Singapore Hong Kong Tokyo
Nairobi Dar es Salaam Cape Town
Melbourne Auckland Madrid

and associate companies in
Berlin Ibadan

Oxford is a trade mark of Oxford University Press

© Bernadette Fitzgerald, Kay Hiatt and Joyce Hilyer 1992
Published by Oxford University Press 1992
Reprinted 1993

A CIP catalogue record for this book is available from the
British Library.

ISBN 0 19 916556 4

Typeset by Pentacor PLC
Printed and bound in Great Britain

Contents

Communication

Message in a picture

Aim: learning that pictures can communicate.

Before people could write they could draw. Some paintings found in caves are thought to date back to about 20,000 B.C. Here are some paintings from France and Spain.

We can read pictures and signs as well as books.

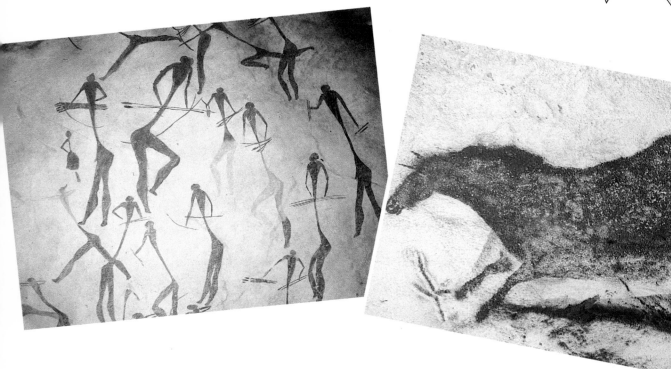

READ ▷
TALK ▷
WRITE ▷

In pairs, look at these paintings and answer these questions.

- What do you think is happening in these paintings?
- Why do you think they were painted?

Write down your answers.

Look for some more pictures of cave paintings. Try your class or school library.

Following on from cave paintings, people started using pictograms. These were very simple pictures drawn to show real things, like this:

rain

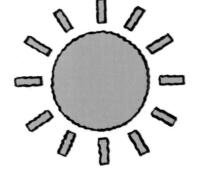

sun

scissors

Make your own pictograms for the following:

house   car   television   tree   robot

Ideograms are ideas which are put into drawings. We use them in signs and symbols today.

Look at these signs and talk with your friend about what they mean.

Make a list of all the signs and symbols you pass on your way home from school.

Communication

Saying it without words

Aim: *learning that we can communicate without words.*

Gestures can communicate.

TALK

ACT

With your friend, talk about what is happening in each picture. No words are being used, yet everyone can understand what is going on.

Take it in turns to try out some of these actions – speaking is *not* allowed.

No!

We scored a goal!

Yes!

Can I have a sweet, please?

Go left!

No! It wasn't me who shouted!

Go right!

READ

TALK

Some people find it difficult to hear and to speak. They can use their fingers to communicate. We call this sign language.

With your friend, look at the pictures below. Try signing some of the letters in the alphabet.

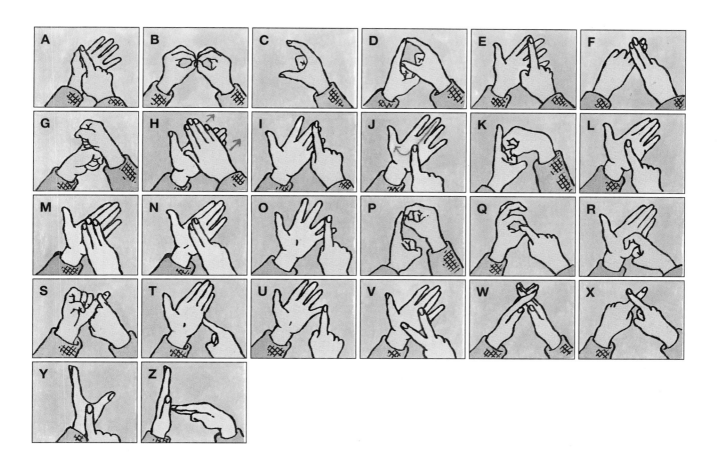

Now practise signing some of these:

Home	Mum	Dad	Dinner	To drink
	tap twice	tap twice		

Communication

Body language

Aim: learning about body language.

READ

Read how this writer describes how Grandpa shows his feelings and even asks questions without saying a word.

Grandpa's face told everything about him. It was always changing from glad to worried to funny to sad. Grandpa could ask a question without saying one word, and even when he was cross with Tamika, his face was a good face, and the look of his mouth and eyes told her that he loved her.

TALK

With a friend, talk about the pictures below. These people are also communicating their feelings without speaking. We call this body language.

WRITE

Copy this chart into your books.

	How the characters feel	Why they feel like this
Picture A	very happy	because she's opening lots of presents
Picture B		
Picture C		
Picture D		

Body language is the language of our faces and bodies.

Now look again at the pictures at the bottom of page 8 and fill in your chart.

You need to describe how the characters feel and why they are feeling like this. Picture A has been done for you.

ACT

In pairs, one of you choose a word from the list below, e.g., angry.

angry

sad

frightened

bored

Now act out, as if you were feeling angry, one of the following:

- making a sandwich
- taking the dog for a walk
- brushing your hair
- unpacking your school bag

Could your friend guess
- what you were doing?
- how you felt?

Now your friend should choose another word from the list and take a turn.

Communication

Writing about feelings

Aim: learning about how writers describe characters' feelings.

READD >

In pairs, read this poem together.

This Morning My Dad Shouted

This morning my dad shouted.
This morning my dad swore.
There was water through the ceiling.
There was water on the floor.
There was water on the carpets.
There was water down the stairs.
The kitchen stools were floating
So were the dining chairs.

This morning I've been crying.
Dad made me so upset.
He shouted and he swore at me
Just 'cause things got so wet.
I only turned the tap on
To get myself a drink.
The trouble is I didn't see
The plug was in the sink.

John Foster

TALK >
ACT >
DRAW >

Now talk about how the characters in this poem are feeling.

Act out *This Morning My Dad Shouted* as a mime.

Draw or paint some pictures about this poem – remember to draw the characters so that they clearly show what they are feeling.

READ >

Read the opening lines below from Hiawyn Oram's book called *Angry Arthur*.

Once there was a boy called Arthur. He wanted to stay up and watch the western on T.V.

'No,' said his mother, 'it's too late. Go to bed.'

'I'll get angry,' said Arthur.

'Get angry,' said his mother.

So he did. Very, very angry.

He got so angry that his anger became a stormcloud exploding thunder and lightning and hailstones.

Which words does the author use to help describe how angry Arthur feels? Draw a picture to go with these words from the story.

Arthur gets more and more angry in the book. See if you can get the book and find out what happens to Arthur.

WRITE >

Can you think of a time when you felt very angry? Write down what happened that day. Share this with your friend or your teacher, or you might like to keep it to yourself.

Story

Parts of a story

Aim: learning about the parts of a story.

All stories have a beginning, a middle and an end.

READ
TALK

In a small group, look at the pictures. Do you know the name of this well-known fairy tale? Try to remember the story and tell it in your own words. Each take a part in turn.

1

2

3

4

5

6

7

8

TALK

Do you like this story?
Say why you like it.

Pictures as well as words can tell a story.

ACT

Act out your favourite parts
of the story together.

Story

Putting a story in the right order

READ
TALK
WRITE

These pictures of the fairy tale *Goldilocks and the Three Bears* are in the wrong order. Say which order they should be in.

1   Start by picking out the picture that shows the beginning of the story. Which letter is beside it? Write the letter down on a piece of paper.
2   Next choose the pictures that show the middle of the story. Again write these letters down.
3   Now write down the letter that shows the end of the story.

A

Next she tried the porridge in Baby Bear's teeny-weeny bowl . . .

B

Finally, feeling tired, she tried Baby Bear's bed and . . .

C

First she saw three chairs . . . she was too heavy for this little chair and as she sat . . .

D

The three bears returned from their walk . . .

E

Once upon a time there were three bears who lived in a cottage in the woods. One morning they made porridge for breakfast but . . .

F

Goldilocks wandered on until she was quite lost. After a while she came to the cottage where the three bears lived. She went in and . . .

G

Goldilocks woke up and how scared she was to see the three bears staring down at her. She jumped out of bed and ran down the stairs and out of the door and . . .

H

That same morning, a little girl called Goldilocks said goodbye to her mother and went for a walk.

TALK
DRAW
WRITE

In your small group, take it in turns to tell the story in the right order. Fill in the missing parts as you tell it.

Now, on your own, choose one of the pictures and make your own drawing or painting of that part of the story.

Write about what is happening in your picture.

Story

The writing pathway

Aim: learning about the stages in a piece of writing.

READ
TALK
WRITE

Now that you have talked about fairy tales, choose either *Goldilocks and the Three Bears* or *Red Riding Hood* to write out in your own words. Don't forget that your story will need a beginning, a middle, and an end. You will need to follow **'The Writing Pathway'** if you want to publish it.

The Writing Pathway

Planning

1 Plan what you are going to say. Share your ideas with a friend.

Drafting

2 Write your first draft on paper or on a word processor.

4 Make any changes to your writing. You can cross things out, add bits, or change the order of what you have written.

Revising

3 Read your writing aloud to a friend. Talk about how you can make it better.

6 Make sure there are no mistakes in your writing.

   a Check that you have spelt all the words correctly.

   b Put in all the capital letters.

   c Put in all the other punctuation, like full stops, commas, and question marks.

Editing

7 Take your work to your teacher for a final check. It has to be correct before you copy it out or print it.

5 Read your writing through again. If you feel you need more help, go back to 3. If you are happy with it, go on to 6.

Publishing

8 Write it out in your best handwriting or print it on a word processor.

Our book of Fairy Tales

DRAW Draw some pictures to illustrate your story.

Story

Characters

Aim: learning more about the characters in stories.

Characters are the people or animals we meet in our stories.

READ
TALK

With a friend, look at these well-known characters from story books.

Can you recognize them?

READ ▷

TALK ▷

With your friend, now read these descriptions of characters. Can you guess who they are?

When I am working I wear a uniform. I take things to people's houses in a big bag.
Who am I? **?**

I am poor although I live in a very big house. I spend all my time cleaning. I have two very ugly sisters.
Who am I? **?**

I am sometimes naughty and don't do as I am told. Once I got lost in a wood. I ended up sleeping in someone else's bed. I am a girl with golden, curly hair.
Who am I? **?**

I am boastful and think I am very clever. Nice juicy children make my mouth water. My skin is green and nobbly. I have sharp teeth that sparkle like 'knives in the sun'. I live on land and in water.
Who am I? **?**

I am an old woman. I have my hair up in a bun. I have a husband, a cat and a dog. I try to be kind to people. There is something very odd about me – I can change size.
Who am I? **?**

I have a long handsome face. I try to be a good father and look after my family. I don't give up easily. Sadly one day I lost my bushy tail. My wife thinks I'm fantastic.
Who am I? **?**

WRITE ▷

Once you think you know who these characters are, write the name of: **a** the character
                                                                        b the story.

You can set it out in a chart like this:

Character	Story	Author

WRITE ▷

READ ▷

Now try to find out who wrote the stories. Add this information to your chart under the heading 'Author'. If you have these books in your classroom, choose one to read and enjoy.

Story

Who am I?

Playing the **'Who Am I?'** game:

TALK

In a small group, make up a set of ten cards, using the names of some of the characters you have already met.

- Each card needs to be 10 cm wide and 5 cm long.
- Print on each card in big letters the name of a character, e.g.:

Baby Bear

Rules of the game

1. Put the cards face down in the centre of the table.

2. The first player picks up a card and silently reads the name of the character written on the card. This player then describes the character out loud, thinking about:

   - What the character looks like
   - how the character dresses
   - what the character does in the story.

Do not say the name of the character or you will spoil the game.

3. This player then says, 'Who am I?'

4. The player who guesses correctly picks up the next card from the pile and the game continues.

5. The game ends when all of the cards have been used up.

DRAW
PAINT
WRITE

Now draw or paint a picture of one of your favourite characters and write a description to go with it.

Give enough clues to help a reader to guess who your character is.
Do not give your character's name.
Remember you can describe:
• what the character looks like
• how the character dresses
• what the character does in the story.
Put in anything that is special about your character.

See how Chris has done it.

Who am I?

I am a good archer.
I am male.
I live in a forest, it is Sherwood Forest.
I am dressed in green.
I have a friend called Little John.
I take from the rich and give to the poor.

Some children put their descriptions of characters into a class **'Who Am I?'** book.

Posters

What's in a poster?

> **Aim: learning how to read a poster.**

READ In pairs, read the poster below.

This poster gives us the following information:

- what is happening (title of the event) — *the end of term concert*
- where it is happening — *Wood Green Primary School*
- when it is happening (date and time) — *July 20th at 6.30 p.m.*
- how much it costs to go in (entrance charge) — *£1 for adults, 50p for children and senior citizens*
- what's on offer (attractions) — *singing, dancing, school orchestra, refreshments*

TALK With your friend, talk about
- who you think would read this poster
- why you think the poster was made.

You can see posters in many places. The poster below was seen outside a library.

TALK
WRITE
READ

With your partner, think of other places where you see posters.

Write a list of these places in your book.

Now, read the poster below.

EASTER STORY TIME
at Stoke Library
on Tuesday 5th April and
Wednesday 6th April
10.45 - 11.45am

FREE! lots of
Stories!

Painting
Competition!
For children
up to 10 years

Fairy Tales

TALK

With a partner, check that the poster above gives you all the important information:
- where it will happen (place)
- what will happen (title of the event)
- the time it will start
- the date
- how much it will cost to go in (entrance charge).

Posters

Write your own!

Aim: learning how to write a poster.

READ

A group of four children talked about a special event that was going to happen in their school. They wanted to make a poster to tell people about it.

First, they planned what would go in their poster. This is how they did it:

Plan for poster

Attractions?
refreshments
lots of stalls
raffle

When is it happening?
date: 2nd July
time: 2pm–4.30pm

making our own poster – school fête

How much will it cost?
75p or £1 adults

Where is it happening?
St. Mark's School

What is happening?
Summer fête

Next each child made a poster. Here is one of them:

TALK

In a small group, talk about a special event that is going to happen in your school: it could be a school disco or Sports' Day. What else could it be?

WRITE

Plan a poster together for this special event.
- Decide what to put on it.
- Find everything you will need to make it, like paper, felt pens, etc.
- When it is finished, decide where to display your poster so that it will be seen by lots of people.

lots of fun – prize raffle!

Summer Fête

at: St. Mark's Primary School

on: Saturday 2nd July

from: 2pm–4.30pm

entrance: 75p for children £1 for adults

Lots of stalls!

Games!

Prizes!

Competitions

READ

This is a photograph of a town crier. Hundreds of years ago, many people were not able to read and write. Then, a town crier was used to tell people what was happening.

ACT

Read your poster out loud, like a town crier would have done. How will you say it?

Writing letters

Letters to friends

Aim: learning to write a letter to a friend.

READ

Letters are set out like this.

> Class 4,
> Parkside Primary School,
> Glasgow
> 4th November, 1992.
>
> Dear Mohammed,
>   In our class
> we've been making safety posters
> for Bonfire Night.
>   I'm going to a Fireworks'
> Party. Are you going to one?
> Tell me if you are.
>
>   Love from
>   Simon

READ

TALK

In pairs, read the letter and talk about:
- who sent the letter
- what it is about
- who will read the letter.

WRITE

Now write your own letter to a friend in another class. Tell your friend about what you are doing today.

Set it out like this:

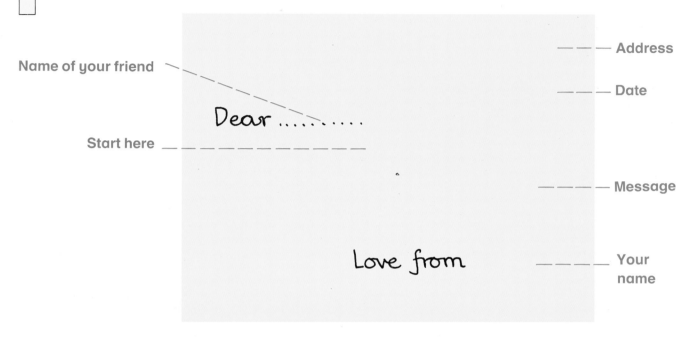

Name of your friend

Address

Date

Dear ....

Start here

Message

Love from

Your name

Ask your teacher if you can make an envelope for your letter. To help you do this, open up a real envelope and see what shape it was before it was stuck together.

When you have made your envelope, put the address on it. Simon addressed his envelope to Mohammed like this:

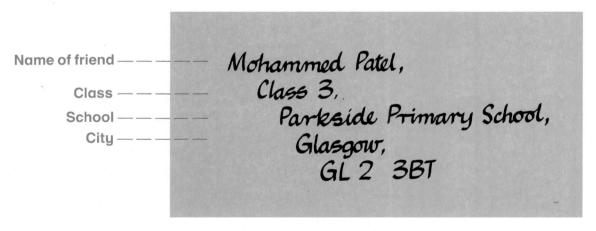

Name of friend — Mohammed Patel,
Class — Class 3,
School — Parkside Primary School,
City — Glasgow,
GL 2 3BT

Write your envelope in the same way.
Now send it to your friend.

Writing letters

Letters from the seasons

Ian McMillan made up letters that the Seasons of the Year could have written to each other.

READ

In a small group, take it in turns to read the letters.

Dear Spring,

It's cold here. The weather has been terrible. It snowed for days and nobody could get out of the house. When it stopped snowing the children went out and built a huge snowman in the corner of the garden. There's still a little bit of snow left in the shade. The new baby stays in the house most of the time, and I can hear her crying.

See you soon,

Yours faithfully,

Winter.

Dear Summer,

It's lovely here. The weather has been fine. It was windy last week, though, and it blew some slates off the house. When the wind dropped the children came out and played in the garden. They've got a sandpit, it's a huge one, and they keep it in the corner by the hedge. The baby sometimes comes out and lies in her pram, and I can hear her laughing.

See you soon,

All the best,

Spring.

Have you noticed how all the letters mention
• what the weather is like
• what the children are doing
• what the baby does.

28

Dear Autumn,

It's hot here. The weather has been lovely. It was so hot last week that some people stayed in the house, where it was cooler. The children came out and played in their paddling pool. It's a huge one, and they've moved the sandpit to fit it in the corner of the garden. The baby sits outside all the time, and I can hear her trying to talk.

See you soon,

Keep smiling,

Summer.

Dear Winter,

It's cool here. The weather has been changing. It's dark in the evenings and the children stay inside. They did come out one evening last week and built a huge bonfire in the corner of the garden where the paddling pool used to be. I see the baby in the house, trying to walk, holding on to furniture.

Don't forget to wrap up warm,

Look after yourself,

See you soon,

Autumn.

WRITE

1 Look at today's date.
   Which season of the year are you in at the moment?
   Try to find a calendar, to help you decide.

2 Write down the name of this season on a piece of paper and underneath brainstorm anything that is special to this time of the year such as:
   • what the weather is like
   • what you wear at this time of year
   • what you have been doing (mention special things happening at school)
   • the games you play.

3 Now write a letter from this season to the next season and describe what is happening. Use the ideas from your brainstorm.

4 Decorate the border of your letter with pictures to show what is happening in your season.

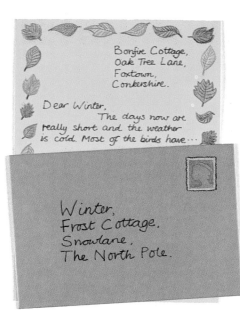

Bonfire Cottage,
Oak Tree Lane,
Foxtown,
Conkershire.

Dear Winter,
     The days now are really short and the weather is cold. Most of the birds have ...

Winter,
Frost Cottage.
Snowlane,
The North Pole.

Writing about ourselves

Everybody's face is different

Aim: learning to choose words to describe ourselves.

READ

Everybody Says

Everybody says
I look just like my mother.
Everybody says
I'm the image of Aunt Bee.
Everybody says
My nose is like my father's
But *I* want to look like *me*!

Dorothy Aldis

The words you use to describe your hair, like **curly, strong, brown, long, shiny,** are called adjectives.

WRITE

Look carefully in a mirror. Write down what you can see. Make some notes about:

your nose   your hair
your mouth   your eyes
the shape of your face.

TALK
WRITE

Share this information with a friend. Does your friend think that you have described yourself well?

Can you now add anything to your notes? Now write a description of your face.

Famous artists often paint pictures of themselves.
You can see some of these self-portraits in art galleries.
Others were painted by children.

TALK
WRITE
DRAW

Which of these portraits is your favourite?

On your own, write a description of the person in the painting. Think carefully about which adjectives you will choose to describe the person.

Draw or paint a picture of your face.
Put your drawing with your description.

Writing about ourselves

As I am now

Aim: learning about each other by asking questions.

Interview time

'. . . and today we're interviewing each other about ourselves . . .'

TALK
WRITE

In pairs, brainstorm a list of questions which will help you to find out more about each other. They can be questions about age, height, languages you speak, favourite foods, and so on.

On your own, write your questions down on a chart like the one which we've started for you below.

Questions to ask my friend	Answers from the interview
1. How old are you?	
2. How many are in your family?	
3. How tall are you?	

Now you are ready to interview each other.

1   First choose which one of you will go first.

2   Ask all of the questions from your chart.

3   Write down your friend's answers.

4   Now the second interview can take place.
    Do it the same way.

5   Use the information to write a description of your
    friend. Alison and Elizabeth wrote their descriptions
    like this.

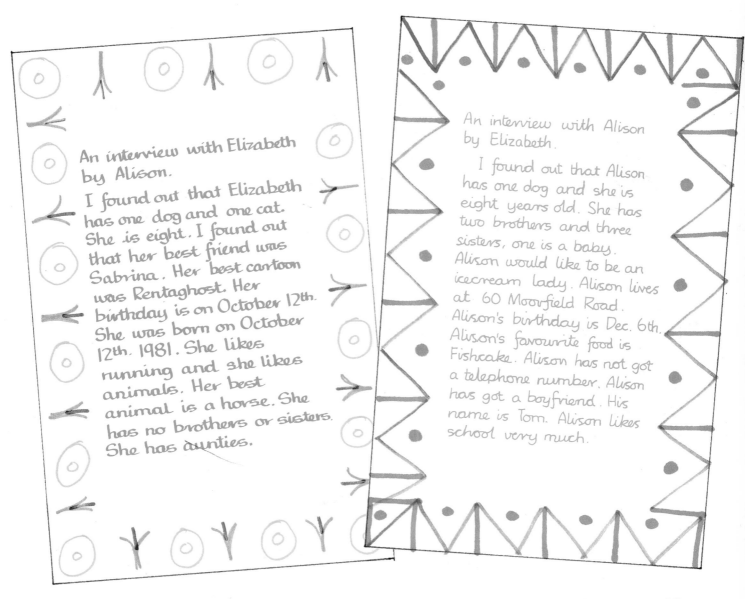

An interview with Elizabeth by Alison.
I found out that Elizabeth has one dog and one cat. She is eight. I found out that her best friend was Sabrina. Her best cartoon was Rentaghost. Her birthday is on October 12th. She was born on October 12th. 1981. She likes running and she likes animals. Her best animal is a horse. She has no brothers or sisters. She has aunties.

An interview with Alison by Elizabeth.
I found out that Alison has one dog and she is eight years old. She has two brothers and three sisters, one is a baby. Alison would like to be an icecream lady. Alison lives at 60 Moorfield Road. Alison's birthday is Dec. 6th. Alison's favourite food is Fishcake. Alison has not got a telephone number. Alison has got a boyfriend. His name is Tom. Alison likes school very much.

Writing about ourselves

Word pictures

READ

With a friend, read and enjoy these descriptions of people:

Savitri was a beautiful princess who lived in India hundreds of years ago. Her eyes were like lotus flowers. Her skin was the colour of sunbeams. Her hair was shining and long and as black as night. Savitri was a very rich princess. Her sarees were made of the very finest silks, and she was always covered in jewels.

From the story **Three Indian Princesses** written by Jamila Gavin.

A sweet little face has Amy
Freckles all over her nose
Eyes that flash with laughter
And cheeks like a pretty pink rose.

Written by Amy's nan.

Mr Smith was quite old but he liked to think that he was quite young. He wore patched jeans and scruffy pullovers, and combed his three hairs right across his head, pretending that the shiny bald skin didn't show through. Once he had started to grow a beard, but as soon as he saw that parts of it were going to be grey, he had shaved it off very quickly.

From the story **Daljit and the Unqualified Wizard** written by Catherine Storr.

His father was tall and lean and wore eyeglasses, except when he was sleeping or in the shower. Mama Green, whose name was Enid, was a short, slim woman with blue-grey eyes and a tiny mouth that always seemed to be on the verge of a smile.

From the story **Chocolate Fever** written by Robert Kimmel Smith.

TALK
DRAW

Which is your favourite description? Can you say why? Read it again.

Now close your eyes. Can you see a picture of this person?

Draw a picture of him or her.

Playing with words

Jokes

READ In a small group, read these jokes aloud to one another.

ouch!

Why are cooks cruel?
Because they beat the eggs and whip the cream.

What do you call a man with a car on his head?
Jack.

What did the big goat say to the little goat?
You can't kid me.

Remember: questions always end with a question mark, like this:
Question: What gets wetter as it dries?
Answer: A towel.

TALK
WRITE
DRAW
Do you know any more jokes like these? Tell your favourite ones to your friends. Make a collection of jokes that really make you laugh. Put them in a class joke book.

Draw some pictures to go with your jokes.

Why did the fly fly?
Because the spider spied her.

Why did the window want to see the doctor?
Because it had a pane.

How does the sea say goodbye?
With a wave.

Why do bees have sticky hair?
Because they use honeycombs.

When does a strawberry need help?
When it is in a jam.

help!

Playing with words

Knock-knock jokes

Enjoy these 'knock-knock' jokes with a partner. Read them aloud together.

Knock-knock.
Who's there?
Ivor.
Ivor who?
Ivor you open the door or
I'll climb through the window.

Knock-knock.
Who's there?
Arthur.
Arthur who?
Arthur any more at home like you?

Knock-knock.
Who's there?
Isabel.
Isabel who?
Isabel necessary on a bike?

38

Knock-knock.
Who's there?
Amos.
Amos who?
A mosquito.

Knock-knock.
Who's there?
Ivor.
Ivor who?
Ivor good mind not to tell you.

Knock-knock.
Who's there?
Justin.
Justin who?
Justin time for a cuppa.

Jokes like these have a special pattern.

WRITE
TALK

Do you know any more 'knock-knock' jokes? Add these to your class joke book. To help you write them down, look again at the jokes on this page. See how they are set out.

If you have a tape recorder, record some of your jokes and play them to another class.

Playing with words

Riddles

Riddles are guessing games.

READ

In pairs read this riddle.

'I'm thinking about something that rhymes with bell
I'm found at the seaside, I'm called a _____ '
(shell)

Did you guess the missing word?

WRITE

Make up some seaside riddles of your own. Follow these instructions:

First copy this chart into your book.

Seaside Word	Rhyming Word
shell	bell
rock	sock
crab	
pool	

Write a seaside word in the first column.
Write a word that rhymes with it in the second column.
Think of as many as you can. The lists are started
for you.
Now you are ready to write your riddles like the one at
the top of the page.

'I'm thinking of something that rhymes with _____
I'm found at the seaside, I'm called a _____ .'

40

READ

Here are some riddles for you to read and puzzle over. If you can't guess the answers then you'll find them at the bottom of the page.

Riddle 1

As I was going to St Ives
I met a man with seven wives.
Each wife had seven sacks
Each sack had seven cats
Each cat had seven kits
Kits, cats, sacks and wives
How many were there going to St Ives?

Riddle 2

Some thing I tell,
With never a word;
I keep it well,
Though it flies like a bird.

Riddle 3

Hold it steady in your hand,
Then you will see another land,
Where right is left, and left is right,
And no sound stirs by day or night.
When you look in, yourself you see,
Yet in that place you cannot be.

Did you get them right?

READ

TALK

Choose a riddle to learn off by heart.
Try it out on your friends.

Answers: **Riddle 1:** one **Riddle 2:** a clock **Riddle 3:** a mirror.

41

Information books

Fiction and non-fiction

> **Aim:** *Learning about the difference between story and information books.*

TALK

With a friend, look at the covers of the books on these two pages, and talk about them.

Which do you think are story books? Why?
Which do you think are information books? Why?

THE Mouse Family Go to the Beach

Pictures by Kazuo Iwamura
by Haruo Yamashita English text by Peggy Blakeley

Adèle Geras
Ritchie's Rabbit

Illustrated by Vanessa Julian-Ottie

ANIMAL LIVES
The Life of a Rabbit

JAN FEDER
ILLUSTRATED BY TILMAN MICHALSKI
TRANSLATED BY ANTHEA BELL

Stories like these which are not true are called fiction.

WRITE

Copy out the chart below.

Now write here the titles of the three story books. The first one is done for you.

Titles of the stories or FICTION BOOKS
1. Ritchie's Rabbit
2.

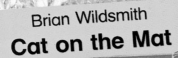

Books which have true information in them are called non-fiction.

WRITE

Make another chart.

Now write the titles of the three information books. The first one is done for you.

Titles of the information or NON-FICTION BOOKS
1. The Life of a Rabbit.
2.

Information books

Information in a picture

Aim: **Learning that pictures can give us information.**

Non-fiction books contain true information.

READ

TALK

With a friend, look at these two pages from information books. Talk together about what you can see in the pictures, then answer the questions below each page.

From **Dogs** by Christine Butterworth.

From **Usborne Spotters' Guide – Cats.**

This dog is looking for people.
The people are trapped by an earthquake.
The dog sniffs to find the people.

Grooming your cat

All cats need regular grooming. It helps keep their coat in good condition and stops them swallowing too much fur when they wash. Short-haired cats should be groomed at least once a week, and long-haired cats every day. It is best to use a soft bristle brush and a metal comb. Get your kitten used to them straight away so it is not frightened and will enjoy being groomed. Even stroking, which all cats enjoy, helps to remove loose fur and gives a shine to the cat's coat.

Groom your cat with a bristle brush

What is the dog wearing on his head? Why?

What is the person doing to the cat? Why?

WRITE

Now make up one of your own questions for each picture. Write it on a piece of paper and ask your friend to write the answer for you.

READ

TALK

Both these pictures below give us more information about mice and rabbits. Talk about these pictures with a friend.

*From **The Mouse in the Barn** by R. Burton.*

The mouse's large round ears are constantly moving to pick up tiny sounds that may mean danger.

*From **The Life of a Rabbit** by Jane Feder.*

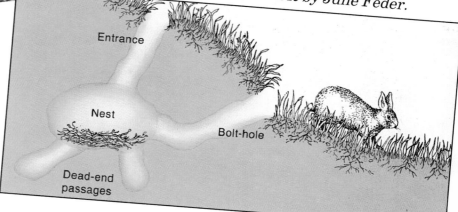

Entrance

Nest

Bolt-hole

Dead-end passages

The Rabbit and its Burrow

TALK

WRITE

Now ask each other questions about each picture. Then list what you have found out. Set it out like this:

The mouse picture
1. The mouse eats nuts.
2. It has . . . .
3. . . . .

The Rabbit and its burrow
1. A rabbit makes a nest .
2. The burrow has . . . .
3. . . . .

Information books

Making your own

READ

In groups of four, you can make a simple information book. Read about how these children made their book. They wanted to make an information book about winter.

First they brainstormed together all the things they knew about winter. Each child used a different coloured felt-tip pen. This is what they wrote.

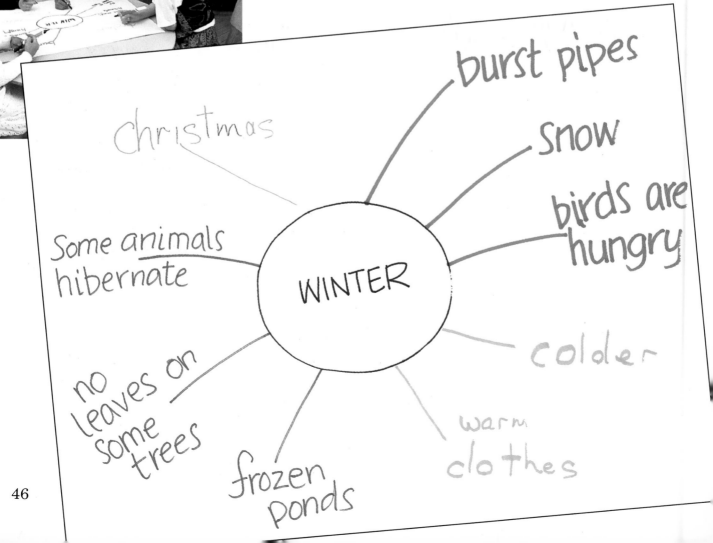

christmas

burst pipes

snow

birds are hungry

Some animals hibernate

WINTER

colder

no leaves on some trees

warm clothes

frozen ponds

46

Then the children decided together which pages each of them would make. They could draw and write in any way they wanted to, but their pages had to contain true information about winter.

Peter put labels on his page.

Susie wrote under her picture.

Then they put their pages together in one big book about winter. The last thing they did was to make the cover. Their book was then placed in the class library.

TALK
WRITE
DRAW

In groups, decide what you would like to make an information book about.

Make one of your own.

Acknowledgements

The publishers would like to thank the following for permission to reproduce copyright material:

Dorothy Aldis, from *Everything and Anything*, © 1925–1929, © renewed 1953–1955 by Dorothy Aldis, by permission of the publishers, the Putnam Publishing Group; **Robert Burton**, from *The Mouse in the Barn*, by permission of Belitha Press Ltd., and Oxford Scientific Films; **Christine Butterworth**, from *Dogs*, by permission of the publishers, Heinemann Publishers (Oxford) Ltd; **John Cunliffe**, two riddles from *Riddles and Rhymes and Rigmaroles* (Deutsch 1971), by permission of Scholastic Publications Ltd.; **Roald Dahl**, from *The Enormous Crocodile* (Cape 1978), illustrated by Quentin Blake, and **Jan Feder**, from *The Life of a Rabbit* (Hutchinson 1982), illustrated by Tilman Michalski, translated by Anthea Bell, both by permission of the Random Century Group; **John Foster**, from *My Blue Poetry Book* (originally Macmillan, now Nelson), by permission of the author; **Jamila Gavin**, from *Three Indian Princesses* (Methuen 1987), by permission of David Higham Associates; **Adèle Geras**, from *Ritchie's Rabbit*, illustrated by Vanessa Julian-Ottie, by permission of the publishers, Hamish Hamilton Ltd.; **Elöise Greenfield**, from *Grandpa's Face* (Hutchinson 1989), by permission of the Random Century Group; **Robert Kimmel-Smith**, from *Chocolate Fever* (Putnam 1972), by permission of David Higham Associates; **Ian McMillan**, 'Letters from the Seasons', first published in this book, © Ian McMillan 1992, by permission of the author; **Hiawyn Oram**, from *Angry Arthur* (1982), illustrated by Satoshi Kitamura, by permission of the publishers, Anderson Press Ltd.; **Alf Prøysen**, from *Little Old Mrs Pepperpot* (Hutchinson 1959), illustrated by David Arthur, by permission of the Random Century Group; **Dr Seuss**, from *The Cat in the Hat* (Collins 1957), by permission of Elaine Greene Ltd.; **Catherine Storr**, from *Daljit and the Unqualified Wizard* (Heinemann 1987), by permission of the Octopus Publishing Group; **Mrs R. Welch**, 'Amy', first published in this book, © Mrs R. Welch 1992, by permission of the author; **Brian Wildsmith**, from *The Cat on the Mat* (1982), by permission of the publishers, Oxford University Press; **Haruo Yamashita**, from *The Mouse Family Go to the Beach* (Hippo), illustrated by Kazuo Iwamura, translated by Peggy Blakely, by permission of A & C Black (Publishers) Ltd.; and material from *The Usborne Spotter's Guide to Cats*, by permission of Usborne Publishing Ltd., London.

The interview pieces on page 33 were written by Alison Sly and Elizabeth Howkins of Brockworth Junior School, Gloucester.

The 'Who Am I?' text on page 21 was written by Chris Evesham of Locking Primary School, Avon.

Photographs: Ancient Art and Architecture Collection p. 4 (both); Bridgeman Art Library p. 31 (top left and bottom right); Kay Hiatt p. 32; Metropolitan Museum of Art, New York, p. 31 (top centre); Graham Paton Gallery, London, p. 31 (bottom left); Syndication International p. 25; John Walmsley pp. 20 (both), 22, 24, 26.

The illustrations are by: Alex p. 31 (bottom, centre), Bucket p. 9, Chris p. 21 (Robin Hood), Bob Dewar pp. 12–13, Paul Dowling pp. 38–39, Elitta Fell pp. 21 and 47, Jane Gedye p. 10, Isobel Morgan Giles pp. 40–41, Robina Green p. 30, Peter Joyce p. 23, Sally Kindberg p. 7, Kimmy McHarrie pp. 28–29 and 34–35, Clare Pound pp. 6 and 8, Graham Round pp. 36–37, Caroline Sharpe p. 18 (Cinderella), Lydia Sherman p. 31 (top right), Mark Southgate pp. 14–15, Pam Stephens pp. 16–17, Tony Wells p. 5, and Jocelyn Wild p. 18 (wolf, bottom right).

The handwriting on pp. 20, 21, 22, 24, 25, 26, 27, 33, 40, 42, 43, 45, and 46 is by Elitta Fell.

The cover illustration is by John Bendall-Brunello.